THE ILLUSTRATED
MOTORCAR LEGENDS
LOTUS

K578 JAH

ROY BACON

PRC

Acknowledgements

The author and publishers wish to acknowledge their debt to all those who loaned material and photographs for this book. The bulk of the pictures are from the extensive archives of the National Motor Museum at Beaulieu. We had kind assistance from Lotus Cars; Cateram Cars and their PR-firm, Brigden Coulter helped with their Sevens; and one picture was supplied by Sotherby's, the auctioneers. Thanks to all who helped.

Copyright © 1995 Sunburst Books
This edition published 1995 by the Promotional Reprint Company Ltd. exclusively for Moa Beckett in New Zealand, Coles in Canada, and Booksales in New York.

ISBN 1 85648 230 8
Printed and bound in China

CONTENTS

EARLY DAYS

Lotus — the product of Colin Chapman's genius, light, quick and highly competitive. Chapman was more than a leader, he was an innovator, technically ahead of the rest, one of the great auto engineers and a pace-setter who was hard but inspiring to work with. His cars began in competition, went on the road, were developed to be among the most exotic and won Formula 1 world titles. In 1992 they even built a world-beating bicycle.

It all began in 1948 in a garage in north London where Chapman built a trials special based on a 1930 Austin 7. It was the first car to carry the Lotus name, and was called the Mark 1, to distinguish it from the 'Special', the usual name of the times. It was soon followed by the Mark 2 which had a Ford 1172cc side-valve engine, Austin 7 chassis in the main, and was trialed and raced. In 1951 the Mark 3 was built for 750 Formula racing — an early inkling of the Chapman approach. He modified the Austin 7 block's inlet system so well that he was very successful in 1951 races and the modification was then banned.

It is hard to believe that the sleek Lotus of the 1990s was conceived by the same man who built this car in 1951 for 750 Formula racing. But even then, Colin Chapman was exploiting the rules so well that they had to be changed. This is his Mark 3.

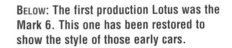

LEFT: Next came the Mark 4. Note the consecutive number plate with the LM no doubt for Lotus Motors. This trials car was built for Michael Lawson in 1952.

BELOW: The first production Lotus was the Mark 6. This one has been restored to show the style of those early cars.

Mark 6 Lotus being driven in a sprint at Brands Hatch in 1956, one of the types of events it was built to compete in.

In 1952 Chapman set up Lotus Engineering in his father's stable in Hornsey, north London. His partner, Michael Allen, became a full-time employee while Chapman kept his day job as a stress engineer and worked evenings and weekends on his cars. The first result was the Mark 4, a trials car built for a client, while the embryo firm moved on to the design of the Mark 6.

First sold in 1953, the Mark 6 was the first production competition Lotus to be built in any numbers, establishing the firm as a small-scale manufacturer. The car was stark and simple in the style of the club racer of the time, but under its simple aluminium panels was a triangulated, tubular space frame far in advance of the beam type in general use. Thus, the cars had both torsional rigidity and little weight, riding on a split Ford front axle giving independent suspension and a Ford rear axle hung on combined coil springs and telescopic dampers.

For the rest of the features, the Mark 6 was largely down to the buyer as it was sold as a kit car to avoid purchase tax. Chapman himself used a 1500cc Ford but owners fitted anything from the 1172cc side-valve Ford upwards. MG engines were popular, but selection was usually made from what was available. The same applied to the gearbox, brakes and wheels — Ford, Austin or MG were common — but the overall result was inevitably the same, a very basic car for road fun and club racing with success.

This is one of the first of the Mark 6 cars to be built and it has enclosed rear wheels to improve Its circuit performance.

By 1953 the firm was re-formed as a limited company with Chapman and Hazel, his wife to be, as directors. The Mark 6 went from strength to strength, over 100 being built in three years. However, the frame and some of the body panels were costly to make, so from the Six came the Seven which was to run on and on into modern times while always remaining a stark, road-legal, racing car.

Before the Seven was launched in 1957 there was the Mark 8 which continued the space frame concept but introduced an aerodynamic body shell. Built for sports-car racing in small numbers in 1954-55, it represented a further step forward and had a De Dion rear axle with inboard drum brakes. The Mark 9 followed in 1955 in the same format but with disc brakes all round on some cars and a variety of engines, while the Mark 10 was created to take a 2-litre Bristol engine.

The end result of this activity was the Eleven which had a new space frame, revised suspension, rack and pinion steering, disc brakes and a handmade aluminium body that was a classic. The fuel tank went on the left and could be supplemented by another on the right for long-distance events, while both front and rear body sections pivoted from the car ends to maximise access.

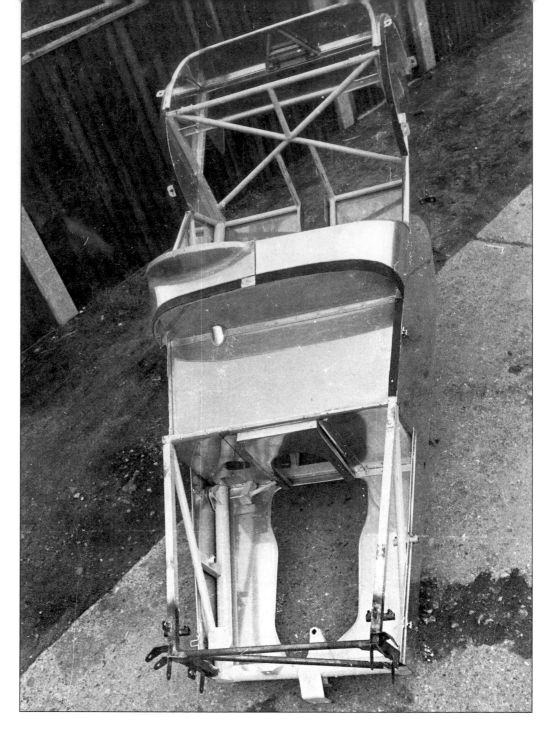

The space frame chassis of the Mark 6 was built of square and round section steel tubing. At this stage the centre body section has been added.

The doors hinged out and down (so could easily be trodden on), and the interior was trimmed. Intended for competition but usable on the road, most cars had a head fairing and driver screen only but a full-width one was listed and mandatory in some races.

Three versions of the Eleven were offered, the Club with Coventry-Climax engines of 1100 or 1500cc; the Sports with the 1172cc side-valve Ford, only three speeds, a beam rear axle and drum brakes; and the Le Mans. The Le Mans was for racing so had the best Climax engines, four speeds, discs, and the best suspension Chapman could devise in 1956, when the cars first appeared.

Thus, in 1957 Lotus offered both a stark and a shapely sports-racing car and were about to add a new model which took them in a totally new direction.

ABOVE: The early cars had split axle front suspension and neat head lamp mounting. The lamp mounting had to be moved when these cars were restored, in order to comply with current regulations.
BELOW: A Mark 6 at Prescott hill climb in 1954 — just the type of event that the car excelled in.

RIGHT: When pressed hard during a race the front wheels of the Lotus would assume these odd angles but the car was fast round the corners.

BELOW: From the Six came the Seven, destined for a very long production run. This one is from 1962 and its Californian number plate is worth noting.

ABOVE: Super sleek lines of the Mark 8, the first of the fully streamlined Lotus models, built in 1954.
BELOW: This is the Mark 9, built in 1955, racing at Aintree in September the same year.

ABOVE: A Mark 9 at Silverstone during 1955, displaying its fine lines and good performance.
BELOW: This is the Mark 10 which was built to take a 2-litre Bristol engine and is seen here at Silverstone in 1971 for a parade on the day of the British Grand Prix.

ABOVE: The Eleven was first built for 1956, with three versions offered. The hinged body sections and drop-down doors were features.
BELOW: An Eleven just ahead of two Sevens during a race at a Silverstone club meeting in 1962.

RIGHT: This Eleven is minus the body to show off its excellent chassis (Earls Court, 1955).

BELOW: Powered by a 1098cc Coventry Climax engine, this Eleven is running at Brands Hatch in 1961.

ABOVE: Brands Hatch in 1957 — an early Eleven running at a club meeting.
BELOW: Early days at Silverstone in a 1956 club event for this Eleven.

ELITE AND ELAN

ABOVE: The 1960 London motor show: an Elite on its stands to raise this low-built car to viewing level for the public. A Formula Junior single-seater is behind on the right.

RIGHT: A 1962 Elite showing off its fine lines and smooth coupe body some years after being built.

In October 1957, at the London motor show, Colin Chapman unveiled the prototype of his new design, the Elite two-seater coupe. It was a sensation for not only was it one of the most stylish cars of the period, it was constructed largely in fibreglass. At that time, most cars using this material retained a tubular chassis and added the body as a shell to give the shape. Chapman's differed completely — the new Lotus in its production form used three large mouldings bonded into one to form both the chassis and body, reinforced by the windscreen hoop and the front suspension frame.

The Elite's body thickness varied to suit the loads it had to bear and the technique resulted in a very light car, weight reduction being a Chapman passion. Under the skin went a 1216cc Coventry Climax overhead camshaft engine fed by one or more carburettors and this drove via a four-speed gearbox to the rear axle. There was independent front suspension by wishbone and spring, and independent rear by Chapman strut which combined with a trailing arm and the drive shaft to locate and control the wheel movement. Disc brakes and wire wheels were fitted and the body had windows which lifted out to be stored, as roll-up ones could not be accommodated.

RIGHT: Rather cramped for working on, this is the hatch of a 1963 Elite with its Coventry Climax engine.

BELOW: Cockpit area of a 1962 Elite showing the simple dash, pleasant interior and low seats.

Inside, the trim was basic and the minimal sound insulation made for a noisy ride. But once on the move, all was forgiven thanks to the handling and the exceptional performance envelope.

To build the Elite, Lotus needed larger premises, and moved to a new factory at Cheshunt in Hertfordshire late in 1959. Sadly, the car proved somewhat unreliable and expensive to build so the firm lost money on all they produced, but it did move them on from being a small competition-car builder to production cars. Early Elites had the combined body and chassis built by a boat firm but during 1960 this activity was taken over by Bristol Aeroplane and some improvements were made to the chassis. The next year the car was available in kit form to save purchase tax and some further changes were made. A few cars were built for racing and altered to suit. By late 1963 production had ended.

Meanwhile, the Seven continued in production and moved to Cheshunt with the firm. It was offered in many forms but all were essentially the same stark racing car with variations in the mechanics. As the years went by these changed to suit what was available so that the cars could always use the latest engines and their optional items.

By the late-1950s, Lotus had started their involvement with Formula 1, at first using front-engined single seaters but progressing to a rear engine in 1960 as Chapman saw that this was the way to go. Success came quickly as Stirling Moss won at Monaco that year, repeating this win in 1961 against strong opposition. In sports-car events, the Eleven and developments from it continued to be successful.

Show time! Maybe on press days, but not something offered on the public days on the Elite or anything else.

An Elite driven by Betty Haig competing in a 1961 hill climb. The nimble handling of the Lotus made it a good vehicle for such events.

Lotus could be thought to have come of age in 1962 when they moved ahead in several areas, away from the problems of the Elite. They unveiled a new car, began to use a new engine, produced a competitive saloon car, and raced a revolutionary Formula 1 car with great success.

Much of this came from a major link forged with Ford as it was one of their engines which became the new unit and powered the Lotus road cars. In essence it was a stock four-cylinder ohv unit fitted with a light-alloy cylinder head carrying twin, chain-driven, overhead camshafts. The capacity began as 1498cc, but was soon raised to 1558cc. There were two twin-choke carburettors and the power went up.

The new car was the Elan which used this engine, had a fibreglass body but used a simple backbone chassis constructed in steel. This carried the engine, close-ratio, four-speed gearbox, rear axle, and the independent suspension for all four disc-braked wheels. Both fixed and drop head bodies were produced, using the same mould, and both had pop-up headlights, limited interior trim and not much noise insulation. Offered in kit form as well as fully assembled, the Elan was beautifully balanced on the road and a real enthusiast's sports-car.

Full frontal of the stark Seven, considered by many to be a four-wheeled motorcycle in the way it performed and dealt with traffic.

Ford of Britain asked Chapman to fit the twin-cam engine into his choice of car from the standard range and build 1,000 of them to homologate the result for competition. The outcome was the famous Lotus-Cortina which took the 1558cc engine, the four-speed gearbox as used in the Elan, had the front suspension uprated and the rear modified, and lost some weight courtesy of light-alloy doors and lids. Finished in white with a green body flash, the car was a success in the sales room and on the circuits.

Finally, Chapman introduced the Lotus 25 into Formula 1 and Jim Clark won three races to take second place in the 1962 championship. In 1963 he won seven and the title. What set the new car apart from its rivals was its mono-coque chassis which saved weight and gave an immensely strong structure in which the engine played its part.

The sports-racing models were nearing the end of their Lotus days by the 1960s, having more than put the firm on the map. Chapman moved firmly into the premier Formula 1 league but did produce the Type 23 for 1962. The works cars were rejected at Le Mans on a dubious technical point (they were likely winners of the Index of Performance — a French domain) so Chapman vowed to ignore the event from then on, which he did. The car itself was cheap in kit form, used a 1097cc Cosworth-Ford, rear-mounted engine in a space frame chassis, and was most successful.

The Seven in 1962 when, as always, it offered outstanding performance but few creature comforts.

Other specialised racing cars followed in many varied formats. These included the Type 27 for Formula Junior, the Type 29 to run at Indianapolis where Clark was second in 1963, the Type 30 for Group 7 sports-car racing using a 4.7-litre Ford V-8 engine, the Type 31 Formula 3 car, and the Type 32 for Formula 2 and the Tasman race series. All of which demonstrated how versatile the firm was, and its ability to solve the problems inherent in many forms of racing.

By 1964 the Formula 1 works car was the Type 33 and Jim Clark used his to good effect in 1965 to again take the world title. He also won at Indianapolis in 1965 using the Type 38 car. However, the Type 40 sports-racing model run that year had little success and demonstrated that Lotus were now stretched too far and attempting too much. It was the last such car and brought to an end the line of sleek, aerodynamic cars that had begun with the Mark 8.

ABOVE: A racing Lotus seen at Thruxton in the 1980s: it was typical of the rear-engined cars that Chapman built for many of the formulae, used over the years.
BELOW: Graham Hill drove for Lotus and won the world title in 1968 but is here seen at the wheel of a Fifteen sports-car some years earlier.

ABOVE: A Lotus Fifteen at Prescott in 1962.
BELOW: On show, the early Elan badged as a 1500, fitted with the 1498cc version of the new four-cylinder, twin overhead camshaft engine. It had fine lines and balance.

CHASSIS SPECIFICATION

Chassis Welded steel backbone type, fully rust proofed.

Front Suspension Unequal length wishbones, independent, coil spring telescopic shock absorbers.

Rear Suspension Fully independent, by wide based wishbones, coil springs and telescopic shock absorbers.

Brakes Hydraulically operated calipers on 9½ inch diameter discs on front wheels. 10 inch diameter discs on rear. Hand brake operating on rear wheels only.

Gearbox Four forward speeds and reverse. Synchromesh on all forward ratios. Oil capacity 1¾ imp. pints (2·1 U.S. pints, 0·99 litres).

Final Drive Chassis mounted hypoid unit, sound insulated. Oil capacity 2 imp. pints (2·4 U.S. pints, 1·13 litres).

Steering Rack and pinion, with telescopic and collapsible steering column. Optional right or left hand drive, 15 inch diameter dished wood-rimmed steering wheel, 2½ turns lock to lock.

Wheels 13 inch diameter special Lotus high speed pressed steel. Four stud fixing. Bright metal hub caps.

Tyres 520 x 13.

ABOVE: Taken from the Elan brochure, this drawing shows the backbone chassis and the method of supporting the engine and suspension systems.

LEFT: Pop-up headlamps of the Elan in their up position. Later cars had a fail safe system in that a fault would leave the lamps up rather than down!

ABOVE: An Elan hardtop doing what so many Lotus cars do so well — compete in club events.
BELOW: The famous Lotus-Cortina which was so successful in concept and execution. An exciting car in its correct white with green side flash.

Fantastic. The great Jim Clark taking the Lotus-Cortina round Brands Hatch as only he knew how. Steering with one wheel well off the ground was no problem to Jim.

EUROPA AND ELAN PLUS 2

The 1970 Lotus Europa which fitted a Renault engine and gearbox from its inception in 1966, reversed to create a mid-engined layout.

While the sports racers were out, the various Formula cars continued to be built for the works and in small numbers for sale, and the stark Seven continued to be offered, its mechanics keeping in step with Ford and Cosworth.

New for the road in 1966 was the Europa, an export market, mid-engined coupe powered by Renault. Lotus took the 1470cc ohv engine plus its four-speed gearbox and drive from the front-wheel-drive Renault 16 and reversed them, giving a good layout for the Europa, good access to the engine, and reduced the Lotus dependence on Ford.

The chassis was a steel backbone, similar in concept to that of the Elan, and the suspension followed the usual Lotus practice, the bolt-on wheels being braked by front discs and rear drums. A very sleek fibreglass body was bonded to the chassis on the early cars, which made accident repair most difficult, and the windows were fixed in place.

LEFT: The Lotus backbone chassis, in this case from an Elan, which provided a ready means for fitting the mechanics at front or rear plus good support for the suspension details.

BELOW: This is the special GKN Europa which was fitted with a Rover V-8 engine to offer a very high top speed to those lucky enough to get to drive it.

The view that most drivers had of the GKN Europa as it sped past them, normally at a high velocity.

A competition version of the Europa was also built in small numbers and this used a 1594cc Lotus-Cosworth twin camshaft engine, five-speed Hewland gearbox, uprated suspension, discs all round, and lost some weight. One car was built for GKN using a Rover V-8 engine and reputedly ran at close to 180 mph. It was used for development work and by some lucky executives.

The Elan had become a Series 2 for 1965 and then a Series 3 fixed-head coupe for 1966 when it was made available in Special Equipment form for either body style. This offered more power, close ratio gears, better brakes and centre-lock wheels as the major changes.

For 1967 the Elan Plus 2 joined the existing models. It had a stretched body and chassis to enable two small rear seats to be added. It kept the twin-cam, Lotus-Ford engine but sported a coupe body whose extra length added to its style.

Meanwhile, the Lotus-Cortina became a Mark 2 but in this form was built by Ford with the stock Cortina rear suspension and was available in any standard Ford colour. Listed up to 1970, it offered an impressive performance and excellent handling.

The Europa was changed to the Series 2 to overcome some of its problems by not bonding the body to the chassis, adding electric windows and improving the interior trim. However, the model remained an export one until 1969 when it finally reached its home market, still available complete or in kit form.

To accommodate a family, Lotus introduced the Elan Plus 2 which included two small seats at the rear, the change enhancing the body lines.

The 1967 year also saw the Formula 1 Type 49 car make its winning debut at the Dutch Grand Prix, Jim Clark at the wheel. This was also the debut for the famous Ford-Cosworth V-8 engine which was to dominate racing for so many years. The car took Graham Hill to a world title in 1968 and continued the development of the monocoque chassis.

During 1968 Lotus gained sponsorship from John Player so ran their team in Gold Leaf red, white and gold colours. From this link came some Elan cars in a matching finish. In the same year the Seven became the Series 3 in various forms, with some changes made to suit parts availability. The Elan became the Series 4 after minor changes. Late in the year the Elan Plus 2 became the Plus 2S with some extra equipment and a better finish. It became the first production Lotus not to be offered as a kit car becaues Chapman wanted to move out of that area. It turned out to be a shrewd move for in 1973 Britain joined the Europeans, VAT replaced purchase tax and the tax advantage of the kit car vanished overnight.

Yet another facet of Lotus in 1968 was the 56, a gas turbine, four-wheel-drive race car built to run at Indianapolis that year. It used a monocoque chassis, a Pratt & Whitney engine and Ferguson transmission to run in the lead until the fuel pump drive failed with just nine laps to the flag.

On the company front there had been another move, for they had outgrown Cheshunt. They moved to Hethel, close to Norwich in Norfolk, where a new factory was created. Lotus became a public company, Chapman was awarded a CBE and, in stages, he directed the firm away from kit cars up-market to faster and more expensive models.

Part of that move centred on the development of a new engine which began when it became known that supplies of the Ford engine block would soon cease. It evolved from the slant-4 Vauxhall unit which was used to speed up development. Its inclination offered a low bonnet line and it soon had twin overhead camshafts and a 16-valve cylinder head plus fuel injection. An alloy block soon followed and the outcome was a 1973cc, four-cylinder engine having a die-cast block, twin camshafts driven by a toothed belt, twin carburettors and 155 bhp. This engine was fitted to the Jensen-Healey and later Jensen cars from 1971-76 which must have helped Lotus to offset the development costs.

A 1971 Europa coupe showing its characteristic body shape and lines.

During the engine development, Lotus built the Type 62 as a Group 6 prototype sports racer. It had a space frame chassis and a body based on the Europa. Finished in Gold Leaf colours it looked, sounded and performed well to indicate areas needing further work. The cars had a short life with the works race team but a least one was sold on and later raced.

In 1970 the Seven was altered into the Series 4 which had a tubular, ladder frame and a fibreglass body moulded in four sections. The result lacked the rigidity of the older models so the handling suffered. The word soon went round and sales were poor. Then came the dreaded VAT on kit cars and in 1973 production ceased. However, this was far from the end as Caterham Car Sales bought the production equipment from Lotus, having been a major and at one time sole dealer for the Seven, and continued with the Series 4. For 1974 they switched to an updated version of the Series 3 which they sold as the Caterham Super Seven.

That simple, stark car continued to run on and offer excitement and it remains available today, usually fitted with a Ford, Rover or Vauxhall engine. Sales were helped by Patrick McGoohan using a Lotus Seven in the cult TV series 'The Prisoner', which was shown around the world many times. This prompted Caterham to offer a replica in 1990 as a limited edition and naturally Patrick received chassis number 6.

In 1967 the Lotus 49 race car and the Ford-Cosworth V-8 engine made a combined debut at the Dutch Grand Prix where Jim Clark took both to the win.

The Ford-Cosworth V-8 engine as installed in the Lotus 49. Both went on to many more successes.

For 1971 the Elan became the S4 Sprint, and the four-seat version, the Plus 2S 130. Both adopted a revised and more powerful engine known as the 'Big Valve', from where the extra came. At the same time the Renault-powered Europa was joined, and then replaced, by the Europa Twin-Cam. This used the Lotus-Ford twin-cam engine which was mated to the four-speed Renault gearbox at first. The racing team had less success in 1971, failing to win a single grand prix, but returned to form the next year when Emerson Fittipaldi took the title.

That was a quiet year for the production cars and 1973 saw the last of the Elan model, the final six of which had a five-speed gearbox. For the Europa Twin-Cam there was the Big Valve engine to create the Europa Special and this drove a five-speed Renault gearbox. The Elan Plus 2 was also offered the option of five speeds using Austin gears which enhanced the car's ability to cruise at speed, but the model was dropped after 1974.

ABOVE: Jim Clark winning the 1967 British Grand Prix at Silverstone in the Lotus 49.

LEFT: A late-1960s sports racing Lotus on a show stand, with typical period lines.

ABOVE: John Player provided Lotus with sponsorship in 1968, resulting in the Gold Leaf team colours of red, white and gold for the 49 race car.
BELOW: Series 3 Seven in the Twin-cam form offered from 1968 to 1970 as the 7SS.

The Elan became the Series 4 in 1968 but the changes were minor. This is a 1970 car.

BELOW: Interior of the Lotus factory with Elan Plus 2 bodies receiving attention.

When finished, the interior of the Elan Plus 2 looked like this.

The 1973cc, four-cylinder Lotus engine which was first used in 1971 and remains the firm's well-developed workhorse. Fitted with twin overhead camshafts and four valves per cylinder from the start, it was later stretched to 2174cc.

ABOVE: John Mills driving the Group 6 Lotus 62 at Silverstone in 1969. The car was based on the Europa body but under that went a space frame chassis.

BELOW: By 1970 the Seven was in Series 4 form which was not so successful. This one is from 1971.

ABOVE: Series 4 Seven which had a fibreglass body and a ladder frame but relatively poor handling by Lotus standards.
BELOW: Caterham Cars took the Seven over and reverted to the Series 3 format. This is a 1983 model fitted with coachwork by Avon of Warwick.

ABOVE: Patrick McGoohan in his role of the 'Prisoner' with the Seven he used in the TV series.

RIGHT: Patrick receiving the keys for chassis 6 of the replica series Caterham built and showed at the 1990 motor show.

ABOVE: Caterham Super Seven in 1991, continuing the long line of simple, stark cars for fun.
BELOW: A 1971 Elan Sprint, and in soft top form.

RIGHT: Engine bay of the Elan Sprint showing the tight fit of the Lotus four-cylinder engine and its ancillaries.

BELOW: Elan Sprint pop-up headlamps in repose, their fit to the body adding to the line.

ABOVE: An Elan S4 Sprint seemingly racing, but actually on test at a circuit.
BELOW: A 1972 Elan with its top down, waiting for driver and passenger to enjoy some fine weather, open-air motoring.

ABOVE: Elan Plus 2 showing off its fine line, made better by the extra length added to get the rear seats in.
BELOW: The 1972 Europa Twin-Cam as shown in the brochure. It used the Lotus-Ford engine in place of the Renault but kept the French gearbox at first.

EuropaTwin Cam

The most distinctive high performance car on the market. Its internationally acclaimed styling and advanced mid-engined design make the Europa unique.

ABOVE: Interior of the 1972 Europa. It shared some items with other models, many common with other marques, to provide Chapman with parts at an acceptable cost.
BELOW: An Elan Sprint in the Gold Leaf colours, a good marketing move used by Lotus and other firms over the years.

ABOVE: Full frontal Elan Sprint as usually seen by other drivers in their mirrors.
BELOW: Drop head coupe Elan Sprint with the hood down for fine weather trips, a 1973 model.

ABOVE: By 1971, the four-seater Elan had become the Plus 2S 130 and was fitted with the 'Big Valve' engine producing more power.
BELOW: A special edition Elan Plus 2 from 1974, its last production year. Such cars were and are built to offer specific extras to entice buyers into the salesroom.

ELITE AND ESPRIT

This 1982 model of the Elite, based on the original 1975 car, introduced a new, crisp body line and much more luxury.

In the middle of 1974 Lotus introduced a new Elite which reached production early in 1975. A good deal different from the 1957 model, the new car was very stylish, sophisticated, expensive and highly distinctive. The concept of a backbone chassis and fibreglass body remained, but the lines were angular in a hatchback form that seated four people in a well-appointed interior. Pop-up headlights were a feature.

The power unit for the Elite was the new 1973cc Lotus engine which was front mounted to drive a five-speed gearbox and thence to the rear wheels. All wheels were alloy and had independent suspension. There were disc brakes at the front and inboard drums at the rear. Such luxury features as air conditioning, power steering, tinted glass, electric windows and a radio all showed how Chapman had moved on from his early concepts.

At the end of 1975 the Europa Twin-Cam model was dropped but the Elite was made available fitted with a three-speed Borg-Warner automatic transmission. It was still a 120 mph vehicle. During the year it was joined by a derivative at first listed as the Eclat. This had the rear of the body restyled to a form more suited to the USA market where the hatchback style failed to find much favour. While the revised body shape was accepted, the name was not and was revised to become the Sprint. This broke with the Lotus tradition that their car names began with the letter 'E' — Chapman had liked the sound of 'Lotus Eleven' which set the style from then on.

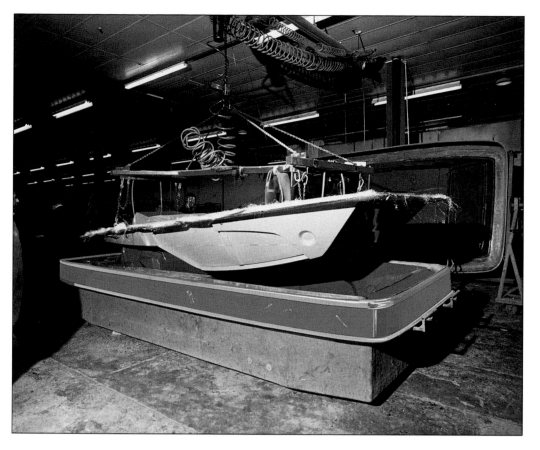

LEFT: The upper body moulding of the Elite, coming out of the mould.

BELOW: Brochure picture of the Eclat which used the Elite body revised at the rear to suit the US market. Later it was renamed the 'Sprint'.

ABOVE: The Lotus Esprit which had great lines and was powered by the Lotus twin-cam engine located aft of the seats. First sold in 1976, this is the 1980 S2 version which was much improved.

RIGHT: Esprit body shell after the two halves have been joined. Now being worked on to trim out the apertures for doors, windows and light units.

While at the 1972 Turin show Chapman saw a Europa carrying a new body styled by Giorgetto Giugario. By 1975 this had been developed into a new Lotus, the Esprit, which made its debut at the Paris show where it was one of the star turns. Stunning and finely balanced lines were much sharper than those of the Europa although the mid-engine concept remained.

Power came from the Lotus 1973cc, twin-cam, 16-valve, four-cylinder engine which drove a five-speed gearbox built in one with the transaxle. The chassis was a steel backbone, longer than the Europa to accommodate a more spacious body interior, and all four wheels had independent suspension and a disc brake.

The Esprit did not reach the public until mid-1976 and immediately ran into trouble. Despite claims for the better, road tests indicated a top speed similar to the Elite, while the cockpit noise level was on a.par with a tractor. Gear changing could be hard, the cooling system was marginal and the vibration level too high for a sophisticated and expensive car. But it did retain the Lotus ability to go round corners very quickly. By the end of 1977 the Esprit was improved to become the S2 version with a change of wheel type and better cooling, but it was still not quiet. The Elite and Eclat, or Sprint, continued alongside it and 1978 proved to be a successful but tragic year for the racing team.

An Esprit having its engine installed. The toothed belt drive to the twin camshafts is clearly seen along with the other drives for alternator and water pump.

The Formula 1 team had enjoyed John Player sponsorship since 1968, first under the Gold Leaf Team Lotus colours, and from 1972 as the JPS or John Player Specials, finished in black with gold lining. Fittipaldi won the title in 1972 and was second in 1973, when the firm retained the constructor's title. Then Lotus began to slip back. This started to change in 1977 when Lotus pioneered ground effect by the use of skirts to seal the car sides to the ground and encourage suction under the car. The effect was immediate. Mario Andretti finished third in the title and won it in 1978. His team mate Ronnie Peterson was second, but tragically crashed on the opening lap at Monza, dying from his injuries that night.

In 1979 Lotus joined with the British part of Chrysler Europe to produce the Sunbeam Lotus. It was built in the mould of the Lotus Cortina and adopted the same strategy. They took the Sunbeam 1300cc body shell, fitted it with the Lotus four-cylinder engine stretched out to 2174cc, and used a five-speed gearbox. Brakes, suspension and tyres were all upgraded to cope with 150 bhp and the result was a small saloon able to reach 125 mph and give its driver much pleasure in the process. Acceleration was dynamic, but the short wheelbase gave nervous handling and a liability to twitch sideways too fast for the average driver to catch. Up to this point, the car would corner with the best. The rally version won its world title in 1981. Chrysler sold the firm to Peugeot around this time and they changed the name to Talbot but allowed production of this exciting model to run on to 1982.

ABOVE: Along each side of the 1978 Esprit Celebratory Edition ran the words 'world champion'.
BELOW: The brochure for the Eclat which showed several views of the car along with all the luggage one could stow in the boot.

Superceding the successful Lotus Elan 2+2, the new Lotus Eclat 2+2 or occasional 4 seat sports car is a logical development combining the performance, comfort and exhilaration expected of a prestige car, with superb handling characteristics synonymous with the name Lotus.

The Eclat design and development programme has included wind tunnel testing at each stage to ensure maximum aerodynamic efficiency and

stability. The Eclat is powered by the highly successful 16 valve, 2 litre, Lotus 907 engine which has set new standards of efficiency, power out-put and endurance.

The Eclat body and interior incorporates the very latest glass fibre reinforced plastic technology and includes the safety features proven in the successful Lotus Elite which was awarded Europe's most coveted safety award,

the Don Safety Trophy.

The luxurious interior is upholstered in washable fabric giving maximum comfort, warmth in Winter and coolness in Summer. Fitted head restraints and deep fully reclining front seats give the driver and passengers superb comfort and thus eliminate fatigue.

The comprehensive instrumentation and control console, including the electric window switches

Esprit S2 from 1980, much improved from the original.

RIGHT AND OPPOSITE: The Lotus 78 in the black and gold of the John Player Special or JPS in which it ran from 1972 on. Mario Andretti won the title in 1978 driving a car of this type which is shown from front, rear and side.

ABOVE: Europa in the JPS colours for 1972 — typical use of the sponsor's finish used to promote sales of the cars and to highlight the sponsor to the public.
BELOW: The Sunbeam Lotus took the small Sunbeam body and fitted it with the Lotus 2174cc engine to create a quick, if twitchy, saloon. Built from 1979 to 1982, it later used the Talbot name.

TURBO ESPRIT

For 1980 Lotus introduced the Turbo Esprit which was to be a true supercar. The engine was the 2174cc four-cylinder, but the addition of a turbocharger to push the power up to 210 bhp meant that it had to be extensively modified internally. It retained carburettors and fitted twin Dell'Orto units — the turbocharger forced air into these rather than the usual layout of sucking through them and blowing into the cylinders.

The Turbo engine drove a five-speed gearbox and transaxle as in the Esprit, but the engine bay was much larger to enable a projected V-8 to be installed. Dry-sump lubrication was used but was changed to the conventional wet system in 1983.

The car was mostly like the Esprit but the rear suspension was revised to isolate it from the body to reduce noise and vibration. The chassis was the proven backbone, modified as needed and the front discs were enlarged. The body concept remained but with a number of amendments which included slats in place of the steeply-raked rear window, but retaining the vertical window behind the seats.

The Turbo Esprit as first built in the Essex colours. It used the 2174cc four-cylinder engine in turbocharged form and the Esprit body in modified form.

ABOVE: The Turbo Esprit in the Essex colours. It adopted slats at the rear in place of the raked window of the stock car.

RIGHT: Interior of the left-hand drive Turbo Esprit which was luxurious and sporting.

The result was an expensive (£20,950 in 1980) car finished in the blue, red and silver of Essex, one of the major race team sponsors. The 100 or so of these built featured a complex audio system and air conditioning. By 1981 the colours were more conventional, and the other features became options which dropped the price to under £17,000 and sales improved.

The Elite, Eclat and Esprit all moved on to S2.2 models during 1980 with the fitment of the 2174cc engine in stock form. The Eclat was also offered as the Riviera model with extras and a modified style thanks to a lift-out roof panel and a rear spoiler. In 1981 the Esprit was further altered to S3 form using the Turbo model chassis and suspension, while the Lotus input into the De Lorean

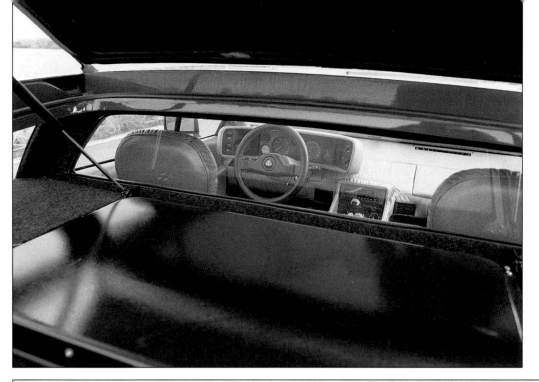

LEFT: View from the rear of the Turbo Esprit with the slatted lid up to show the inside window just behind the seats.

BELOW: Out on the road with the twin pop-up headlights up and on to warn other traffic that there is a Turbo Esprit coming up fast.

project was completed. They had to turn a concept into a practical two-seater coupe in two years which they did. Despite their technical success, the scheme was a commercial disaster which became a scandal.

On the grand prix front Lotus had dropped back but Chapman's innovative skills produced the twin-chassis concept. This allowed the suspension to be softer to give the driver an easier time and avoided the dangers that arose should a body skirt fail. There were protests as to the eligibility of the car and although it ran in practice, it was never raced.

Lotus did not regain the grand prix initiative despite having the talents of Nigel Mansell (1980-84), Ayrton Senna (1985-87) and Nelson Piquet (1988-89) among others. Only Senna won any races, third in the championship in 1987 was his best year.

The engine bay was enlarged for the Turbo Esprit but was still well filled.

It was in 1983 that Lotus first announced their active suspension system which replaced the conventional springs with hydraulic actuators. These were powered by a pressure pump via a valve controlled electronically by an on-board computer. It was 1987 before the system reached their Formula 1 car, by which time they had Honda power, Senna at the wheel and a couple of wins.

By 1981 Lotus were struggling with much reduced sales despite price cuts, because of the recession, the De Lorean crisis, distribution problems in the USA, and trouble with an American Express loan. Chapman reduced the workforce, was forced to do consultancy work for other firms, and brilliantly forged a link with Toyota to use their components in exchange for his expertise.

It proved to be a difficult time but, late in 1982, the Elite was dropped and the Eclat replaced by the Excel which used a Toyota gearbox, disc brakes and drive shafts. The body style had some amendments and the price was reduced which helped sales.

Then tragedy struck — on 16th December 1982 Anthony Colin Bruce Chapman suffered a fatal heart attack at the age of 54. The innovative genius had gone, leaving his firm with a clear problem-solving approach and positive outlook. The firm was shaken to its core but soon pulled itself together to continue car production and consultancy work for others. In October 1984 Lotus exhibited their Etna at the British motor show. This was a concept car, styled by Giugiaro and powered by a Lotus 4-litre, V-8 engine pushing out some 320 bhp. Late in 1985 the Excel became the Excel SE fitted with a high compression version of the 2174cc engine which produced 180 bhp. There were new spoilers front and rear, plus a new dash and interior. Behind the scenes a new Elan was under development but then, early in 1986, came a takeover bid from General Motors, the world's largest car company. Accepted, it gave Lotus both the money it needed and much larger consulting contracts.

In 1987 the blown car reversed its name to Esprit Turbo and had some changes to improve power delivery rather than output. Listed as the HC, it was short-lived as a much-revised version was introduced late that year. That year also saw the Excel SA, with a four-speed automatic transmission, join the SE version.

The Turbo Esprit in 1982.

The revised Esprit was unveiled in October 1987 to reveal a new body of composite construction using Kevlar to reinforce the fibreglass. Built using the Lotus vacuum-assisted resin injection process, the result was consistent in both quality and weight with a high finish. The body style was subtly altered to be less aggressive, smoother and more suggestive of understated quality.

It had the backbone chassis, independent suspension, disc brakes – ventilated at the front, and the well-proven 2174cc four-cylinder engine. For the basic car this gave 172 bhp, or 215 bhp in turbo form, the latter figure rising to 228 bhp for the US Federal, low-emission version. For all, the transaxle and five-speed gearbox came from Renault.

During 1989 the Esprit Turbo was offered in SE form. For this the power was raised to 264 bhp by adding fuel injection and what Lotus called a charge-cooler. This was a water cooling system with radiator which cooled the ingoing air to enhance engine efficiency. This was high despite running on unleaded fuel under the restriction of a catalytic converter, and the car easily complied with the harshest of emission laws. The SE had the front suspension revised to make its response more constant under changing conditions.

ABOVE: During 1980 the Elite fitted the 2174cc engine and was then listed as the S2.2 model. This one is from 1982.
BELOW: Nice lines of the 1982 Elite S2.2 which continued to offer a high performance to owners.

LEFT: Interior of the 1982 Elite which differed from the other Lotus cars but kept the concept of placing the instruments in front of the driver.

BELOW: The Lotus factory in 1981 with an Eclat in the foreground. The good factory lighting helped quality control.

ABOVE: Another section of the factory, well back down the assembly line to where the engine unit joined the backbone chassis.
BELOW: The Eclat in its Riviera form, in which it came with some extras as standard, plus a discreet name on the side panel at the rear.

ABOVE: Front view of the Eclat Riviera which used the 2.2-litre engine.
BELOW: An Eclat in reverse at the factory in 1981, receiving its final touches before bagging up for delivery.

The Lotus-Esprit Series 3 is probably the best known mid-engined production two-seater car in Britain and one of the world's most exciting sports cars. The 1985 version has many improvements that make it even more desirable.

The sheer power of the Lotus 2.2 litre, light alloy 16 valve engine which develops 160 bhp, thrusts you from 0-60 mph in only 6.7 seconds – and on to a top speed of 138 mph! Yet with all this power, the Esprit Series 3 has proved to be amazingly economical 'in service', providing 38.7 mpg at a constant 56 mph, aided in no small degree by its elegant Giugiaro styled, aerodynamically efficient shape. The superbly sleek lines produce a drag co-efficient of only 0.33 – and the specially reinforced high tensile composite body is completely immune to corrosion. Its futuristic lines are matched by impeccable paintwork that now has matching bumpers, rear light plinths and mirror housings.

The gleaming body houses an immensely strong protective cage to ensure occupant protection – whilst the hot-dip galvanised backbone chassis (which carries an 8 year guarantee against corrosion) protects the life and durability of your car long after others have succumbed.

Like the engine – the suspension, steering and brakes benefit from lessons learned in the hard world of Formula One racing. In fact, both the suspension and the ventilated front disc brakes on this '85 model are completely new, whilst the race proven Goodyear NCT-VR tyres are now of an improved compound designed to give a better grip on wet surfaces, making for improved control, roadholding and powerful progressive stopping.

The luxurious interior has deep cushioned seats with body-hugging foam foundations, comprehensive controls and instrumentation providing a sumptuous and ergonomic environment for both driver and passenger alike. Full or partial "Connolly" hide interior is available as an optional extra and could add the finishing touch to this superlative machine.

The fully carpeted luggage compartment now has increased capacity and the facility to house the optional glass sunroof. Additional stowage capacity is available under the bonnet.

The Lotus Esprit Series 3 only needs servicing at 6000 mile intervals and carries with it a full 12 months unlimited mileage warranty. With top marks in every department the 1985 Esprit Series 3 has to be a 'must' for the sporting driver.

ABOVE: The brochure for the 1985 Series 3 Esprit. This version adopted the Turbo model chassis and suspension from 1981.
BELOW: Rear view of the Series 3 Esprit of 1982 on a damp day.

ABOVE: The Lotus racing workshop from where so many trend-setting cars set out over the years.
BELOW: Brochure picture of the Elite in its 1985 form, still fitted with the 2.2-litre engine and retaining its style.

ABOVE AND OPPOSITE: A special edition Turbo Esprit built for 1982 as the St Tropez. It had an open, soft-top body and a special rear-end treatment to accommodate this when folded. The front of the car remained in stock form, including the concealed headlights.

A new look for the 1984 Lotus Excel
The Lotus Excel body shape has taken on a more aggressive look, with a carefully designed rear spoiler providing even greater stability at high cruising speeds, and four visually distinctive louvres on the bonnet. Bumpers, sills, logos and coachlining have all been colour co-ordinated to further emphasise this new look.

In contrast, the interior exudes a feeling of calm. Lotus now offer a choice of two cloth trims (brushed or ribbed velour) as well as their top quality hide option. New rear seat styling, redesigned door pillars which give improved air extraction and reduced wind noise, and a new sports steering wheel complete the interior changes for 1984, allowing for absolute control in complete comfort.

ABOVE: This brochure shows the 1985 Excel, which replaced the Eclat in 1983, and used some Toyota parts.
BELOW: The Esprit as for 1985: the model continued alongside the Turbo version.

1985 Lotus Esprit Turbo

The Lotus Esprit Turbo – the most sought after mid-engined two-seater production car in Britain – and probably the worlds most exciting sports car, is now even more enjoyable – thanks to the 1985 specification.

Sink into the luxurious cockpit. Put your foot down. Feel the thrilling surge of power emanating from the superb Lotus 2.2 litre, light alloy 16 valve, turbo charged engine as you leap from 0-60 mph in a mere 5.5 seconds! You can continue accelerating up to 152 mph where speed restrictions allow!

In addition to its acknowledged power, the Lotus Esprit Turbo has a host of matching qualities. The beautifully sleek aerodynamic body styled by Giugiaro produces a drag co-efficient of only 0.33 and helps to make the Esprit Turbo surprisingly economical on fuel. Its gleaming paintwork – now enhanced by matching bumpers and door mirror housings, covers a specially reinforced composite body shell that is completely immune to corrosion.

This in turn houses an immensely strong protective cage to ensure occupants safety, whilst a hot-dip galvanised backbone chassis adds tremendous overall strength and now carries an 8 year guarantee against corrosion.

The Lotus-designed suspension, steering and braking system are the result of our long association with Formula One racing. Indeed, the '85 Esprit Turbo has an entirely new front suspension system and now incorporates ventilated front disc brakes. Specially formulated Goodyear NCT-VR tyres with a change of compound give improved grip and roadholding combined with excellent ride and handling characteristics.

All this, plus 12 months unlimited mileage warranty and 6000 mile service intervals, makes the Esprit Turbo the most complete performance vehicle on the road today.

The brochure for the 1985 Turbo Esprit.

LEFT AND FOLLOWING PAGE: Views of the Turbo Esprit from above, side and rear to show off its fine lines which changed little over the years.

ABOVE: The Etna concept car styled by Giugiaro and seen late in 1984 at the British motor show. It was fitted with a V-8 Lotus engine.
BELOW: Interior of the Etna followed the Lotus format but with added Italian flair and the Giugiaro label at the base of the steering wheel.

RIGHT: The Lotus V-8 engine which was two banks of their four on a common crankcase, which meant that most of the Lotus engine development still applied.

BELOW: An Excel as for 1985, before it took the SE format.

Lotus Eminence

ABOVE: Yet another consulting job was this Lotus Eminence, a far cry from their usual line of cars.
BELOW: For 1987 the name changed to Esprit Turbo and it was coded as the HC model, which stood for high compression.

1948 LOTUS 1988

Handling, performance and style.

ABOVE: This photograph in the 1988 brochure celebrated the 40 years of Lotus. Everything is there: sports cars, racing cars, tuned saloons and the production line of luxury grand tourers.

RIGHT: This is a Lotus Four engine on test in 1988, with its turbocharger and exhausts being monitored for temperature.

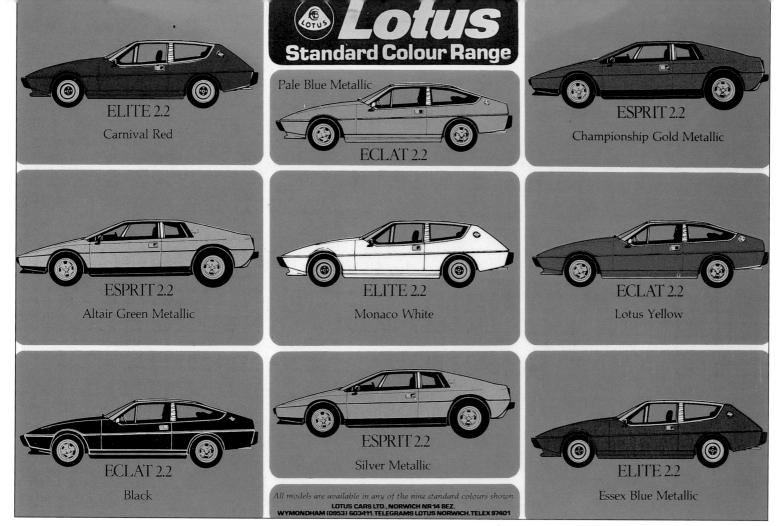

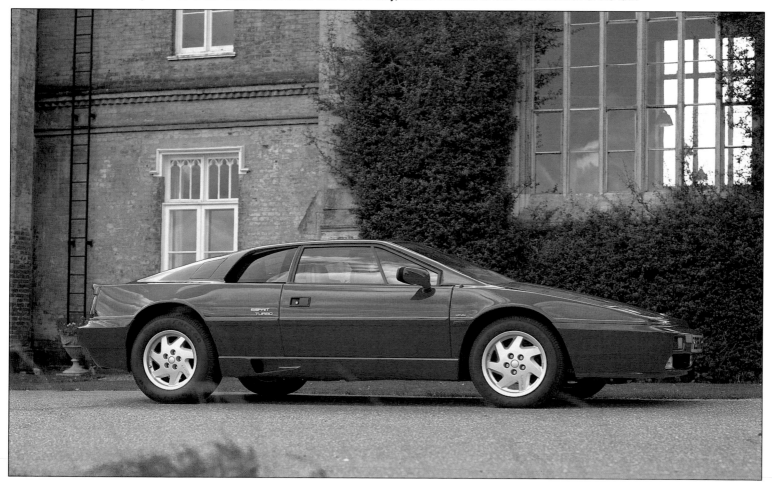

ABOVE: This colour chart for 1988 was so much better than the usual colour chip samples for showing the cars in the finish.
BELOW: This is the 1989 Esprit Turbo in the carnival red which sets it off nicely, even if inclined to draw the attention of the law.

ABOVE: The same Esprit Turbo in red showing its frontal aspect and very sleek lines.

ABOVE: From the rear, the Esprit Turbo shows no weakness, its fine lines portraying function as well as style.

LEFT: Interior of the Esprit Turbo with its short, stubby gear lever among all the home comforts.

ABOVE: Parked on Westminster Bridge at 7.25am for a quick picture before the traffic and wardens catch it.
BELOW: This Esprit Turbo is out in the country, well away from the tiresome city traffic for which it is not suited.

ELAN AND ESPRIT

ate in 1989 the long-awaited Elan joined the Esprit and Excel to take Lotus back into the open two-seater market. Originally conceived back in 1981 to use a Toyota engine, this changed to a Japanese Isuzu unit, as General Motors had a stake in that firm. Lotus engineers would have preferred a Vauxhall engine, known to be a good unit, but this did not fit GM's needs. However, the 1588cc four-cylinder, 16-valve, twin-overhead camshaft unit had fuel injection and with or without turbo, it responded well to some Lotus development.

What set the Elan apart for Lotus was the use of front-wheel drive. And what set it apart from other marques using that system was a patented raft subframe front suspension system that gave it unmatched road handling. For the rest there was the backbone chassis, a five-speed gearbox, disc brakes, pop-up headlamps and a soft top that was quick and easy to raise or lower. Technically brilliant but, sadly, too expensive when it finally reached the public in 1990, the Elan was also costly to make so made no profit for Lotus.

The range ran on for 1990 when the firm once again put some excitement into a stock saloon. The result was the Lotus Carlton, called the Lotus Omega outside the UK, respectively right and left-hand drive versions of the Vauxhall Carlton fitted with its own or the Opel Senator 3-litre, six-cylinder, 24-valve engine enlarged to 3615cc. To this Lotus added their own cylinder head having 24 larger valves, and twin overhead camshafts, the power enhanced by twin turbo-chargers.

In 1990, Lotus brought back the Elan to return to the open two-seater market. Its engine was a 1588cc Japanese Isuzu four-cylinder unit with twin overhead camshafts and four valves per cylinder.

The Elan on the Lotus stand at the 1989 Earls Court show. It broke new ground for the firm as it used front-wheel drive along with a special front suspension system.

A six-speed gearbox was used along with ventilated disc brakes while the suspension systems, front and rear, were worked over by Lotus as only they knew how. The result was a very fast, 165 mph, saloon with excellent handling.

For 1991 the Esprit S3 had a power boost thanks to the fitment of the 215 bhp turbo engine, the Esprit Turbo became the Esprit S with 228 bhp and the SE ran on. All had the option of ABS brakes. The Elan and Excel models continued alongside the Esprit and into 1992, but in the middle of the year both were dropped from the Lotus range along with the Carlton/Omega. At the Frankfurt show in 1991, Lotus showed another concept car, the M200, a speedster based on the Elan.

Only the base Esprit and the SE version continued for 1992, sporting a new rear spoiler and revised front bib which improved the aerodynamics. In October 1992 a LotusSport Esprit X180R won a title in the USA. This competition version of the Esprit paid dividends for the production cars. For 1993 the SE became the S4 and gained power steering. It was joined by two other vehicles of very different forms. First was the Esprit Sports 300 which was a limited production car intended to be a basis for international GT racing with just 50 built each year. To that end the engine power was pushed up to 300 bhp while some weight was lost despite the addition of metal braces to the body to strengthen it. Provision was made for a racing roll cage.

The second vehicle demonstrated the technical abilities of the Lotus companies for it was a very special track-pursuit bicycle, the LotusSport, priced at a cool £15,000. It was in truth a replica of the one ridden to a gold medal at the 1992 Olympics by Chris Boardman in the 4000-metre race. The frame was an aerofoil section moulded in carbon-composite with titanium inserts at the load points. Lotus skills in monocoque forms in those materials, plus their other skills, resulted in this impressive achievement. In July 1993 the pursuit cycle was joined by the LotusSport 110 road model which debuted in the Tour de France and on which Boardman won a stage in the 1994 race.

Front view of the new Elan, which was technically brilliant but costly to build.

August 1993 brought a surprising turn of events for Group Lotus was bought from General Motors by Bugatti Industries, an unprecedented move. In September a further concept model, the E-Auto. It was a four-seat saloon with minimal fuel consumption. The computer simulation predicted 140 mpg!

Lotus moved on into 1994 with the Esprit in S4 and Sport 300 forms while the engineering and consultancy parts of the group continued to solve problems for firms large and small. In March, at Geneva, the Elan returned to the range in S2 form as a limited production run of 800 cars. For these the wheel size was increased to 16-inch, the turbocharged engine fitted and some detail changes made to the body style and fitments.

In addition to the Super Seven, Caterham introduced their Caterham 21 for 1995, yet another 'Back to the Future' exercise. This differed from the Seven in its sleek, aerodynamic body so revived memories of the Lotus Eleven while the power came from Ford, Rover or Vauxhall engines.

New from 1995 was the S4s version of the Esprit which used the turbocharged 2174 cc engine revised to raise both power and torque. The body had wheel arch extensions added to cover the tyres and an improved interior.

The Esprit S4 ran on for 1995 with the revised interior while the Sport 300 and Elan S2 continued in the lists. Sales were up for the year following the takeover and a Bugatti was on the Lotus stand at the late 1994 British Motor Show, indicative of further expansion and new business.

Thus both Lotus and Caterham kept to the Chapman design concept of more for less.

ABOVE: Elan with the pop-up lights on and up. An expensive car to buy, it still made Lotus no profit due to its costs and had a short production life.
BELOW: This 1989 Excel fell victim to the recession and was dropped after 1992.

ABOVE: This Lotus Carlton saloon, also built as the Lotus Omega with left-hand drive, was based on the Vauxhall model. Fitted with a 3615cc engine, twin overhead camshafts and twin turbochargers, it was good for 165 mph.

BELOW: By 1993 the Esprit Turbo was in S4 form and had gained a rear spoiler and power steering.

RIGHT: Interior of the S4 Esprit Turbo which had moved on with the times to reflect changing needs.

BELOW: Close up of the rear spoiler on the S4 Esprit Turbo, a useful addition to a very fast car and needed to ensure good rear wheel grip at speed.

The S4 Esprit Turbo with the lamps up and on main beam to light its path.

ABOVE: This is the 1994 style for the S4 Esprit Turbo which continued the fine line and style of the first of the series.
BELOW: In 1993 the firm introduced the Lotus Esprit Sport 300 as a limited production car. It had less weight and more power for immense road performance or competition use. This is the 1994 model.

ABOVE: The Elan returned in S2 form for 1994 as a short production run of 800 cars. It used the turbocharged engine and had some detail changes.
BELOW: At Dartford, Caterham Cars kept producing the Super Seven. Here it is standing in front of a line of early Lotus cars.

RIGHT: The 1992 Super Seven Sprint by Caterham Cars which faithfully kept to the early Colin Chapman ideal.

BELOW: The sleek Caterham 21, introduced at the late 1994 British Motor Show to evoke memories of the Lotus Eleven.

ABOVE: The Esprit S4s was introduced at the late 1994 British Motor Show to offer an enhanced performance above that of the base S4.
BELOW: The LotusSport 110 road bicycle that made its debut in the 1994 Tour de France. Not cheap but technically highly advanced.

LOTUS MODELS

SPORTS, TRIALS AND RACING MODELS

MODEL	YEAR	CC	ENGINE	BODY
Mark 1	1948	747	Austin	trials
Mark 2	1949-50	1172	Ford	trial/race
Mark 3	1951-52	747	Austin	racing
Mark 4	1952	1172	Ford	trials
Mark 6	1952-55	various		sports
Mark 7	1957-60	various		sports
Mark 7 Series 2	1960-67	various		sports
Mark 7 Series 3	1968-70	various		sports
Mark 7 Series 4	1970-73	various		sports
Caterham Seven	1973-date	various		sports
Mark 8	1954	various		sports racing
Mark 9	1955	various		sports racing
Mark 10	1955	2000	Bristol	sports racing
Eleven Club	1956-58	various		sports racing
Eleven Sports	1956-58	various		sports racing
Eleven Le Mans	1956-58	various		sports racing
Eleven Series 2	1957-58	various		sports racing
15	1958-60	1500/2000	Climax	sports racing
17	1959	750	Climax	sports racing
19	1960-62	2500	Climax	sports racing
23	1962-64	1097	Cosworth	sports racing
30 Group 7	1964-65	4700	Ford	sports racing
40	1965	5300	Ford	sports racing
X180R	1992		Lotus	sports racing

PRODUCTION ROAD MODELS

MODEL	YEAR	CC	ENGINE	BODY
Elite Series 1	1957-60	1216	Climax	coupe
Elite Series 2	1960-63	1216	Climax	coupe
Elite S.2 Super	1962-63	1216	Climax	coupe
Elan Series 1	1962-64	1558	Lotus-Ford	open/coupe
Elan Series 2	1965	1558	Lotus-Ford	open/coupe
Elan Series 3	1965-67	1558	Lotus-Ford	open/coupe
Elan Series 4	1968-70	1558	Lotus-Ford	open/coupe
Elan S4 Sprint	1971-73	1558	Lotus-Ford	open/coupe
Elan Plus 2	1967-68	1558	Lotus-Ford	coupe
Elan Plus 2S	1968-70	1558	Lotus-Ford	coupe
Elan Plus 2S 130	1971-74	1558	Lotus-Ford	coupe
Elan Plus 2S 130/5	1972-74	1558	Lotus-Ford	coupe
Lotus-Cortina	1963-66	1558	Lotus-Ford	saloon
Lotus-Cortina 2	1967-70	1558	Lotus-Ford	saloon

MODEL	YEAR	CC	ENGINE	BODY
Europa	1966-67	1470	Renault	coupe
Europa Series 2	1967-71	1470	Renault	coupe
Europa Twin-Cam	1971-75	1558	Lotus-Ford	coupe
Elite	1974-80	1973	Lotus	coupe
Elite S2.2	1980-82	2174	Lotus	coupe
Eclat (Sprint)	1975-80	1973	Lotus	coupe
Eclat S2.2	1980-82	2174	Lotus	coupe
Eclat Riviera	1980-82	2174	Lotus	coupe
Sunbeam Lotus	1979-81	2174	Lotus	saloon
Esprit	1975-77	1973	Lotus	coupe
Esprit S2	1977-80	1973	Lotus	coupe
Esprit S2.2	1980	2174	Lotus	coupe
Esprit S3	1981-93	2174	Lotus	coupe
Turbo Esprit	1980-86	2174	Lotus	coupe
Esprit Turbo HC	1987	2174	Lotus	coupe
Esprit Turbo	1988-90	2174	Lotus	coupe
Esprit S	1991	2174	Lotus	coupe
Esprit Turbo SE	1989-92	2174	Lotus	coupe
Esprit S4	1993-date	2174	Lotus	coupe
Esprit S4s	1995	2174	Lotus	coupe
Esprit Sport 300	1993-date	2174	Lotus	coupe
Excel	1982-85	2174	Lotus	coupe
Excel SE	1986-92	2174	Lotus	coupe
Excel SA	1987-92	2174	Lotus	coupe
Elan	1990-92	1588	Isuzu	open
Elan SE	1990-92	1588	Isuzu	open
Elan S2	1994-date	1588	Isuzu	open
Lotus Carlton	1990-92	3615	Vauxhall	saloon
Lotus Omega	1990-92	3615	Vauxhall	saloon

FORMULA CARS

MODEL	YEAR	FORMULA	CC	ENGINE
12	1957-59	1 & 2	various	
16	1958-59	1 & 2	various	
18	1960	1	2500	Coventry-Climax
20	1961	Junior	1000	Cosworth Ford
21	1961	1	1500	Coventry-Climax
22	1962	Junior	1100	Cosworth Ford
24	1962	1	1500	Coventry-Climax
25	1962-65	1	1500	Coventry-Climax
27	1963	Junior	1100	Cosworth Ford
29	1963	Indianapolis	4200	Ford
31	1964	3	1000	various
32	1964	2	1000	Cosworth
32	1964	Tasman	2500	Coventry-Climax
33	1964-65	1	1500	Coventry-Climax
34	1964	Indianapolis	4200	Ford
35	1965	2 & 3	1000	Cosworth
38	1965	Indianapolis	4200	Ford

MODEL	YEAR	FORMULA	CC	ENGINE
39	1966	Tasman	2500	Coventry-Climax
41	1966-68	2 & 3	various	Cosworth
42	1967	Indianapolis	4200	Ford
43	1966-67	1	3000	BRM
44	1966	2	1000	Cosworth
48	1967	2	1600	Cosworth
49	1967-70	1	3000	Cosworth Ford
51	1967-68	Ford	1600	Ford
55	1968	3	1000	various
56	1968	Indianapolis	turbine	
56B	1971	gas turbine		
59	1969	3	1000	Holbay Ford
59B	1969	2		Cosworth
59F	1970	Ford	1600	Ford
61	1969	Ford	1600	Ford
62	1969	Prototype	2000	Lotus
63	1969	1	3000	Cosworth
64	1969	Indianapolis	2600	Ford
68	1969	A	5000	Ford
69	1970-71	2 & 3	1600	Cosworth
69F	1970-71	Ford	1600	Ford
70	1970	F5000 & A	5000	Ford
72	1970-75	1	3000	Cosworth
73	1972	3	1000	Ford
74	1973	2	2000	Lotus
76	1974	1	3000	Cosworth
77	1976	1	3000	Cosworth
78	1977-78	1	3000	Cosworth
79	1978-79	1	3000	Cosworth
80	1979	1	3000	Cosworth
81	1980-81	1	3000	Cosworth
86	1980	1	3000	Cosworth
87	1981	1	3000	Cosworth
88	1981	1	3000	Cosworth
91	1982	1	3000	Cosworth
92	1983	1	3000	Cosworth
93	1983	1	1500	Renault
94	1983	1	1500	Renault
95	1984	1	1500	Renault
96	1984	CART	2600	Cosworth
97	1985	1	1500	Renault
98	1986	1	1500	Renault
99	1987	1	1500	Honda
100	1988	1	1500	Honda
101	1989	1	3500	Judd
102	1990-92	1	3500	Lamborghini
107	1992-94	1	3500	Ford
109	1994	1	3500	Honda